This Journal Belongs to:

_____

_____

_____

Trading Rules

Trading Rules

Trading Rules

Trading Rules

Trading Rules

Trading Rules

TRADING GOALS

Month: _____

Notes: _____
_____
_____
_____
_____
_____
_____
_____
_____

MONTHLY TRADING PLAN AND STRATEGY

Plan:_____

_____

_____

_____

_____

_____

_____

_____

_____

Strategy used :_____

_____

_____

_____

_____

_____

_____

_____

_____

_____

_____

Goals Achieved? ◯ Yes   ◯ No

TRADING LOG

Month										
Trade Type	Stocks ◯ Options ◯ Future ◯ Others ◯ _____									
Market Condition										
Balance										

No	Date	Name/Symbol	Time	Currency Pair	Qty	Price	Entry	Exit	Loss/ Profit	Ratio / %

Notes:_____
_____
_____
_____
_____
_____
_____
_____
_____
_____
_____
_____
_____
_____
_____
_____
_____
_____
_____
_____
_____
_____
_____
_____
_____
_____
_____
_____
_____

TRADING LOG

Month

Trade Type   Stocks ◯   Options ◯   Future ◯   Others ◯ _____

Market Condition

Balance

No	Date	Name/Symbol	Time	Currency Pair	Qty	Price	Entry	Exit	Loss/ Profit	Ratio / %

Notes:_____
_____
_____
_____
_____
_____
_____
_____
_____
_____
_____
_____
_____
_____
_____
_____
_____
_____
_____
_____
_____
_____
_____
_____
_____
_____
_____
_____
_____
_____
_____

TRADING LOG

Month

Trade Type Stocks ◯ Options ◯ Future ◯ Others ◯ _____

Market Condition

Balance

No	Date	Name/Symbol	Time	Currency Pair	Qty	Price	Entry	Exit	Loss/ Profit	Ratio / %

Notes:_____

TRADING LOG

Month

Trade Type Stocks ○ Options ○ Future ○ Others ○ _____

Market Condition

Balance

No	Date	Name/Symbol	Time	Currency Pair	Qty	Price	Entry	Exit	Loss/ Profit	Ratio / %

Notes:_____

TRADING GOALS

Month: _____

Goals of the month

Notes:_____

_____

_____

_____

_____

_____

_____

_____

MONTHLY TRADING PLAN AND STRATEGY

Plan:_____

_____

_____

_____

_____

_____

_____

_____

_____

_____

_____

Strategy used :_____

_____

_____

_____

_____

_____

_____

_____

_____

_____

_____

_____

_____

Goals Achieved? ◯ Yes   ◯ No

Notes:_____

TRADING LOG

Month

Trade Type   Stocks ◯ Options ◯ Future ◯ Others ◯ _____

Market
Condition

Balance

No	Date	Name/Symbol	Time	Currency Pair	Qty	Price	Entry	Exit	Loss/ Profit	Ratio / %

Notes:_____
_____
_____
_____
_____
_____
_____
_____
_____
_____
_____
_____
_____
_____
_____
_____
_____
_____
_____
_____
_____
_____
_____
_____
_____
_____
_____
_____
_____
_____
_____
_____
_____

TRADING LOG

Month

Trade Type Stocks ⭕ Options ⭕ Future ⭕ Others ⭕ _____

Market Condition

Balance

No	Date	Name/Symbol	Time	Currency Pair	Qty	Price	Entry	Exit	Loss/ Profit	Ratio / %

Notes:_____

_____

_____

_____

_____

_____

_____

_____

_____

_____

_____

_____

_____

_____

_____

_____

_____

_____

_____

_____

_____

_____

_____

_____

_____

_____

_____

_____

_____

_____

_____

_____

_____

TRADING LOG

Month											
Trade Type	Stocks ◯		Options ◯	Future ◯	Others ◯	_____					
Market Condition											
Balance											

No	Date	Name/Symbol	Time	Currency Pair	Qty	Price	Entry	Exit	Loss/ Profit	Ratio / %

Notes:_____
_____
_____
_____
_____
_____
_____
_____
_____
_____
_____
_____
_____
_____
_____
_____
_____
_____
_____
_____
_____
_____
_____
_____
_____
_____
_____
_____
_____
_____
_____
_____
_____

TRADING GOALS

Month: _____

Goals of the month

Notes:_____
_____
_____
_____
_____
_____
_____
_____

MONTHLY TRADING PLAN AND STRATEGY

Plan:_____
_____
_____
_____
_____
_____
_____
_____
_____
_____
_____

Strategy used :_____
_____
_____
_____
_____
_____
_____
_____
_____
_____
_____
_____
_____

Goals Achieved? ◯ Yes   ◯ No

Notes:_____

TRADING LOG

Month

Trade Type Stocks ○ Options ○ Future ○ Others ○ _____

Market Condition

Balance

No	Date	Name/Symbol	Time	Currency Pair	Qty	Price	Entry	Exit	Loss/ Profit	Ratio / %

Notes:_____

TRADING LOG

Month

Trade Type Stocks ◯ Options ◯ Future ◯ Others ◯ _____

Market Condition

Balance

No	Date	Name/Symbol	Time	Currency Pair	Qty	Price	Entry	Exit	Loss/ Profit	Ratio / %

Notes:_____

TRADING LOG

Month _____

Trade Type Stocks ◯ Options ◯ Future ◯ Others ◯ _____

Market Condition

Balance

No	Date	Name/Symbol	Time	Currency Pair	Qty	Price	Entry	Exit	Loss/ Profit	Ratio / %

Notes:_____
_____
_____
_____
_____
_____
_____
_____
_____
_____
_____
_____
_____
_____
_____
_____
_____
_____
_____
_____
_____
_____
_____
_____
_____
_____
_____
_____
_____
_____

TRADING GOALS

Month: _____

Goals of the month

Notes:_____
_____
_____
_____
_____
_____
_____
_____
_____

MONTHLY TRADING PLAN AND STRATEGY

Plan:_____

_____

_____

_____

_____

_____

_____

_____

_____

_____

Strategy used :_____

_____

_____

_____

_____

_____

_____

_____

_____

_____

_____

_____

Goals Achieved? ◯ Yes ◯ No

Notes:_____
_____
_____
_____
_____
_____
_____
_____
_____
_____
_____
_____
_____
_____
_____
_____
_____
_____
_____
_____
_____
_____
_____
_____
_____
_____
_____
_____
_____
_____
_____
_____

TRADING LOG

Month

Trade Type   Stocks ○ Options ○ Future ○ Others ○ _____

Market Condition

Balance

No	Date	Name/Symbol	Time	Currency Pair	Qty	Price	Entry	Exit	Loss/Profit	Ratio / %

Notes:_____

_____

_____

_____

_____

_____

_____

_____

_____

_____

_____

_____

_____

_____

_____

_____

_____

_____

_____

_____

_____

_____

_____

_____

_____

_____

_____

_____

_____

_____

TRADING LOG

Month

Trade Type   Stocks ◯   Options ◯   Future ◯   Others ◯ _____

Market Condition

Balance

No	Date	Name/Symbol	Time	Currency Pair	Qty	Price	Entry	Exit	Loss/ Profit	Ratio / %

Notes:_____

TRADING LOG

Month	
Trade Type	Stocks ⃝ Options ⃝ Future ⃝ Others ⃝ _____
Market Condition	
Balance	

No	Date	Name/Symbol	Time	Currency Pair	Qty	Price	Entry	Exit	Loss/ Profit	Ratio / %

Notes:_____
_____
_____
_____
_____
_____
_____
_____
_____
_____
_____
_____
_____
_____
_____
_____
_____
_____
_____
_____
_____
_____
_____
_____
_____
_____
_____
_____
_____
_____
_____

TRADING GOALS

Month: _____

Goals of the month

Notes:_____
_____
_____
_____
_____
_____
_____
_____
_____

MONTHLY TRADING PLAN AND STRATEGY

Plan:_____
_____
_____
_____
_____
_____
_____
_____
_____
_____
_____

Strategy used :_____
_____
_____
_____
_____
_____
_____
_____
_____
_____
_____
_____
_____
_____

Goals Achieved? ◯ Yes   ◯ No

Notes:_____

TRADING LOG

Month

Trade Type Stocks ◯ Options ◯ Future ◯ Others ◯ _____

Market Condition

Balance

No	Date	Name/Symbol	Time	Currency Pair	Qty	Price	Entry	Exit	Loss/ Profit	Ratio / %

Notes:_____

TRADING LOG

Month

Trade Type Stocks ⭕ Options ⭕ Future ⭕ Others ⭕ _____

Market Condition

Balance

No	Date	Name/Symbol	Time	Currency Pair	Qty	Price	Entry	Exit	Loss/ Profit	Ratio / %

Notes:_____
_____
_____
_____
_____
_____
_____
_____
_____
_____
_____
_____
_____
_____
_____
_____
_____
_____
_____
_____
_____
_____
_____
_____
_____
_____
_____
_____
_____

TRADING LOG

Month

Trade Type   Stocks ◯ Options ◯ Future ◯ Others ◯ _____

Market Condition

Balance

No	Date	Name/Symbol	Time	Currency Pair	Qty	Price	Entry	Exit	Loss/ Profit	Ratio / %

Notes:_____
_____
_____
_____
_____
_____
_____
_____
_____
_____
_____
_____
_____
_____
_____
_____
_____
_____
_____
_____
_____
_____
_____
_____
_____
_____
_____
_____
_____
_____

TRADING GOALS

Month: _____

Goals of the month

Notes:_____

_____

_____

_____

_____

_____

_____

_____

MONTHLY TRADING PLAN AND STRATEGY

Plan:_____

_____

_____

_____

_____

_____

_____

_____

_____

Strategy used :_____

_____

_____

_____

_____

_____

_____

_____

_____

_____

_____

_____

_____

Goals Achieved? ◯ Yes   ◯ No

Notes:_____

TRADING LOG

Month

Trade Type Stocks ◯ Options ◯ Future ◯ Others ◯ _____

Market Condition

Balance

No	Date	Name/Symbol	Time	Currency Pair	Qty	Price	Entry	Exit	Loss/ Profit	Ratio / %

Notes:_____
_____
_____
_____
_____
_____
_____
_____
_____
_____
_____
_____
_____
_____
_____
_____
_____
_____
_____
_____
_____
_____
_____
_____
_____
_____
_____
_____
_____
_____
_____
_____

TRADING LOG

Month

Trade Type   Stocks ◯   Options ◯   Future ◯   Others ◯ _____

Market Condition

Balance

No	Date	Name/Symbol	Time	Currency Pair	Qty	Price	Entry	Exit	Loss/ Profit	Ratio / %

Notes:_____
_____
_____
_____
_____
_____
_____
_____
_____
_____
_____
_____
_____
_____
_____
_____
_____
_____
_____
_____
_____
_____
_____
_____
_____
_____
_____
_____
_____
_____
_____
_____

TRADING LOG

Month

Trade Type   Stocks ◯   Options ◯   Future ◯   Others ◯ _____

Market Condition

Balance

No	Date	Name/Symbol	Time	Currency Pair	Qty	Price	Entry	Exit	Loss/ Profit	Ratio / %

Notes:_____
_____
_____
_____
_____
_____
_____
_____
_____
_____
_____
_____
_____
_____
_____
_____
_____
_____
_____
_____
_____
_____
_____
_____
_____
_____
_____
_____
_____
_____
_____
_____
_____

TRADING GOALS

Month: _____

Goals of the month

_____
_____
_____
_____
_____
_____
_____
_____
_____
_____
_____
_____
_____
_____
_____
_____
_____
_____

Notes:_____
_____
_____
_____
_____
_____
_____
_____
_____

MONTHLY TRADING PLAN AND STRATEGY

Plan:_____
_____
_____
_____
_____
_____
_____
_____
_____
_____

Strategy used :_____
_____
_____
_____
_____
_____
_____
_____
_____
_____
_____
_____
_____

Goals Achieved? ◯ Yes   ◯ No

Notes:_____

TRADING LOG

Month

Trade Type Stocks ◯ Options ◯ Future ◯ Others ◯ _____

Market Condition

Balance

No	Date	Name/Symbol	Time	Currency Pair	Qty	Price	Entry	Exit	Loss/ Profit	Ratio / %

Notes:_____
_____
_____
_____
_____
_____
_____
_____
_____
_____
_____
_____
_____
_____
_____
_____
_____
_____
_____
_____
_____
_____
_____
_____
_____
_____
_____
_____
_____
_____
_____

TRADING LOG

Month

Trade Type   Stocks ◯   Options ◯   Future ◯   Others ◯ _____

Market Condition

Balance

No	Date	Name/Symbol	Time	Currency Pair	Qty	Price	Entry	Exit	Loss/ Profit	Ratio / %

Notes:

TRADING LOG

Month

Trade Type Stocks ◯ Options ◯ Future ◯ Others ◯ _____

Market Condition

Balance

No	Date	Name/Symbol	Time	Currency Pair	Qty	Price	Entry	Exit	Loss/ Profit	Ratio / %

Notes:_____

TRADING GOALS

Month: _____

Goals of the month

_____
_____
_____
_____
_____
_____
_____
_____
_____
_____
_____
_____
_____
_____
_____
_____

Notes:_____
_____
_____
_____
_____
_____
_____
_____

MONTHLY TRADING PLAN AND STRATEGY

Plan:_____

_____

_____

_____

_____

_____

_____

_____

_____

_____

_____

Strategy used :_____

_____

_____

_____

_____

_____

_____

_____

_____

_____

_____

_____

Goals Achieved? ◯ Yes   ◯ No

Notes:_____

TRADING LOG

Month

Trade Type Stocks ◯ Options ◯ Future ◯ Others ◯ _____

Market Condition

Balance

No	Date	Name/Symbol	Time	Currency Pair	Qty	Price	Entry	Exit	Loss/ Profit	Ratio / %

Notes:_____
_____
_____
_____
_____
_____
_____
_____
_____
_____
_____
_____
_____
_____
_____
_____
_____
_____
_____
_____
_____
_____
_____
_____
_____
_____
_____
_____
_____
_____
_____

TRADING LOG

Month

Trade Type Stocks ◯ Options ◯ Future ◯ Others ◯ _____

Market Condition

Balance

No	Date	Name/Symbol	Time	Currency Pair	Qty	Price	Entry	Exit	Loss/ Profit	Ratio / %

Notes:_____

TRADING LOG

Month

Trade Type   Stocks ◯   Options ◯   Future ◯   Others ◯ _____

Market Condition

Balance

No	Date	Name/Symbol	Time	Currency Pair	Qty	Price	Entry	Exit	Loss/ Profit	Ratio / %

Notes:_____
_____
_____
_____
_____
_____
_____
_____
_____
_____
_____
_____
_____
_____
_____
_____
_____
_____
_____
_____
_____
_____
_____
_____
_____
_____
_____
_____
_____
_____
_____
_____

TRADING GOALS

Month: _____

Goals of the month

(blank lined list)

Notes: _____

_____

_____

_____

_____

_____

_____

_____

_____

MONTHLY TRADING PLAN AND STRATEGY

Plan:_____

_____

_____

_____

_____

_____

_____

_____

_____

_____

Strategy used :_____

_____

_____

_____

_____

_____

_____

_____

_____

_____

_____

_____

_____

Goals Achieved? ◯ Yes   ◯ No

Notes:_____

TRADING LOG

Month

Trade Type Stocks ◯ Options ◯ Future ◯ Others ◯ _____

Market Condition

Balance

No	Date	Name/Symbol	Time	Currency Pair	Qty	Price	Entry	Exit	Loss/ Profit	Ratio / %

Notes:_____

TRADING LOG

Month

Trade Type Stocks ○ Options ○ Future ○ Others ○ _____

Market Condition

Balance

No	Date	Name/Symbol	Time	Currency Pair	Qty	Price	Entry	Exit	Loss/ Profit	Ratio / %

Notes:_____

TRADING LOG

Month

Trade Type Stocks ◯ Options ◯ Future ◯ Others ◯ _____

Market Condition

Balance

No	Date	Name/Symbol	Time	Currency Pair	Qty	Price	Entry	Exit	Loss/ Profit	Ratio / %

Notes:

TRADING GOALS

Month: _____

Goals of the month

Notes:_____
_____
_____
_____
_____
_____
_____
_____

MONTHLY TRADING PLAN AND STRATEGY

Plan:_____

_____

_____

_____

_____

_____

_____

_____

_____

Strategy used :_____

_____

_____

_____

_____

_____

_____

_____

_____

_____

_____

_____

Goals Achieved? ◯ Yes   ◯ No

Notes:_____
_____
_____
_____
_____
_____
_____
_____
_____
_____
_____
_____
_____
_____
_____
_____
_____
_____
_____
_____
_____
_____
_____
_____
_____
_____
_____
_____
_____

TRADING LOG

Month											
Trade Type	Stocks ◯ Options ◯ Future ◯ Others ◯ _____										
Market Condition											
Balance											

No	Date	Name/Symbol	Time	Currency Pair	Qty	Price	Entry	Exit	Loss/ Profit	Ratio / %

Notes:_____
_____
_____
_____
_____
_____
_____
_____
_____
_____
_____
_____
_____
_____
_____
_____
_____
_____
_____
_____
_____
_____
_____
_____
_____
_____
_____
_____
_____
_____
_____
_____
_____

TRADING LOG

Month

Trade Type   Stocks ○ Options ○ Future ○ Others ○ _____

Market Condition

Balance

No	Date	Name/Symbol	Time	Currency Pair	Qty	Price	Entry	Exit	Loss/ Profit	Ratio / %

Notes:_____
_____
_____
_____
_____
_____
_____
_____
_____
_____
_____
_____
_____
_____
_____
_____
_____
_____
_____
_____
_____
_____
_____
_____
_____
_____
_____
_____
_____
_____
_____

TRADING LOG

Month

Trade Type   Stocks ○   Options ○   Future ○   Others ○ _____

Market Condition

Balance

No	Date	Name/Symbol	Time	Currency Pair	Qty	Price	Entry	Exit	Loss/ Profit	Ratio / %

Notes:_____
_____
_____
_____
_____
_____
_____
_____
_____
_____
_____
_____
_____
_____
_____
_____
_____
_____
_____
_____
_____
_____
_____
_____
_____
_____
_____
_____
_____
_____
_____

TRADING GOALS

Month: _____

Goals of the month

_____
_____
_____
_____
_____
_____
_____
_____
_____
_____
_____
_____
_____
_____
_____
_____

Notes:_____
_____
_____
_____
_____
_____
_____
_____

MONTHLY TRADING PLAN AND STRATEGY

Plan:_____

_____

_____

_____

_____

_____

_____

_____

_____

_____

Strategy used :_____

_____

_____

_____

_____

_____

_____

_____

_____

_____

_____

_____

_____

Goals Achieved? ◯ Yes   ◯ No

Notes:_____

TRADING LOG

Month

Trade Type Stocks ⃝ Options ⃝ Future ⃝ Others ⃝ _____

Market Condition

Balance

No	Date	Name/Symbol	Time	Currency Pair	Qty	Price	Entry	Exit	Loss/ Profit	Ratio / %

Notes:_____
_____
_____
_____
_____
_____
_____
_____
_____
_____
_____
_____
_____
_____
_____
_____
_____
_____
_____
_____
_____
_____
_____
_____
_____
_____
_____
_____
_____

TRADING LOG

Month

Trade Type   Stocks ○ Options ○ Future ○ Others ○ _____

Market Condition

Balance

No	Date	Name/Symbol	Time	Currency Pair	Qty	Price	Entry	Exit	Loss/ Profit	Ratio / %

Notes:_____
_____
_____
_____
_____
_____
_____
_____
_____
_____
_____
_____
_____
_____
_____
_____
_____
_____
_____
_____
_____
_____
_____
_____
_____
_____
_____

TRADING LOG

Month

Trade Type Stocks ○ Options ○ Future ○ Others ○ _____

Market Condition

Balance

No	Date	Name/Symbol	Time	Currency Pair	Qty	Price	Entry	Exit	Loss/ Profit	Ratio / %

Notes:_____
_____
_____
_____
_____
_____
_____
_____
_____
_____
_____
_____
_____
_____
_____
_____
_____
_____
_____
_____
_____
_____
_____
_____
_____
_____
_____
_____
_____
_____
_____

TRADING GOALS

Month: ____________

Goals of the month

Notes:

MONTHLY TRADING PLAN AND STRATEGY

Plan:_____

_____

_____

_____

_____

_____

_____

_____

_____

_____

Strategy used :_____

_____

_____

_____

_____

_____

_____

_____

_____

_____

_____

_____

Goals Achieved? ◯ Yes   ◯ No

Notes:_____
_____
_____
_____
_____
_____
_____
_____
_____
_____
_____
_____
_____
_____
_____
_____
_____
_____
_____
_____
_____
_____
_____
_____
_____
_____
_____
_____
_____
_____
_____
_____

TRADING LOG

Month

Trade Type Stocks ○ Options ○ Future ○ Others ○ _____

Market Condition

Balance

No	Date	Name/Symbol	Time	Currency Pair	Qty	Price	Entry	Exit	Loss/ Profit	Ratio / %

Notes:_____
_____
_____
_____
_____
_____
_____
_____
_____
_____
_____
_____
_____
_____
_____
_____
_____
_____
_____
_____
_____
_____
_____
_____
_____
_____
_____
_____
_____
_____
_____
_____
_____
_____
_____
_____

TRADING LOG

Month

Trade Type Stocks ◯ Options ◯ Future ◯ Others ◯ _____

Market Condition

Balance

No	Date	Name/Symbol	Time	Currency Pair	Qty	Price	Entry	Exit	Loss/ Profit	Ratio / %

Notes:_____
_____
_____
_____
_____
_____
_____
_____
_____
_____
_____
_____
_____
_____
_____
_____
_____
_____
_____
_____
_____
_____
_____
_____
_____
_____
_____
_____

TRADING LOG

Month

Trade Type Stocks ◯ Options ◯ Future ◯ Others ◯ _____

Market Condition

Balance

No	Date	Name/Symbol	Time	Currency Pair	Qty	Price	Entry	Exit	Loss/ Profit	Ratio / %

Notes:_____

Notes

Notes

Notes

Notes

Made in the USA
Las Vegas, NV
21 February 2022